Watch It Grow

A Butterfly's Life

Nancy Dickmann

Heinemann Library
Chicago, Illinois

www.capstonepub.com
Visit our website to find out more information about Heinemann-Raintree books.

To order:
☎ Phone 800-747-4992
💻 Visit www.capstonepub.com to browse our catalog and order online.

Edited by Rebecca Rissman, Nancy Dickmann, and Catherine Veitch
Designed by Joanna Hinton-Malivoire
Picture research by Mica Brancic
Production by Victoria Fitzgerald
Originated by Capstone Global Library Ltd Library
Printed and bound in the United States of America in North Mankato, Minnesota. 102013   007822RP

15 14 13
10 9 8 7 6 5 4 3

Library of Congress Cataloging-in-Publication Data
Dickmann, Nancy.
 A butterfly's life / Nancy Dickmann. -- 1st ed.
   p. cm. -- (Watch it grow)
 Includes bibliographical references and index.
 ISBN 978-1-4329-4138-3 (hc) -- ISBN 978-1-4329-4147-5 (pb) 1.
Butterflies--Life cycles--Juvenile literature. I. Title. II. Series: Dickmann, Nancy.
Watch it grow.
 QL544.2.D53 2010
 595.78'9--dc22
                          2009049152

Acknowledgments
We would would like to thank the following for permission to reproduce photographs: iStockphoto pp. **14** (© Carla Vaughan), **15** (© Lowell Gordon), **17** (© Ron Brancato), **18** (© Olivier Blondeau), **20** (© Jill Lang) **22 bottom** (© Carla Vaughan), **23 top** (© Lowell Gordon); Nature Picture Library p. **16** (© Rolf Nussbaumer); Photolibrary pp. **4** (First Light Associated Photographers/© Peter Reali), **8** (Animals Animals/Breck P Kent), **9** (Tips Italia/John T Fowler), **10** (Oxford Scientific (OSF)/© Brian Kenney), **22 top** (Animals Animals/Breck P Kent); Shutterstock pp. **5** (© Cathy Keifer), **6** (© Cathy Keifer), **7** (© GJS), **11** (© Lori Skelton), **12** (© James A. Kost), **13** (© Cathy Keifer), **19** (© Cheryl Casey), **21** (© sjgh), **22 right** (© Cathy Keifer), **22 left** (© GJS), **23 middle top** (© Cathy Keifer), **23 bottom** (© Cathy Keifer), **23 middle bottom** (© Cheryl Casey).

Front cover photograph (main) of a monarch butterfly on a red flower reproduced with permission of Shutterstock (© Doug Lemke). Front cover photograph (inset) of a monarch caterpillar eating milkweed reproduced with permission of iStockphoto (© Ron Brancato). Back cover photograph of a monarch chrysalis reproduced with permission of iStockphoto (© Lowell Gordon).

The publisher would like to thank Nancy Harris for her assistance in the preparation of this book.

Every effort has been made to contact copyright holders of material reproduced in this book. Any omissions will be rectified in subsequent printings if notice is given to the publisher.

Contents

Life Cycles

All living things have a life cycle.

Butterflies have a life cycle.

A caterpillar hatches from an egg.

It turns into a butterfly.

A butterfly lays eggs.

The life cycle starts again.

Eggs and Caterpillars

egg

A butterfly lays eggs on a leaf.

A tiny caterpillar is inside each egg.

The caterpillar hatches from the egg.

The caterpillar eats the egg.

The caterpillar eats leaves.

Growing and Changing

The caterpillar grows too big for its skin.

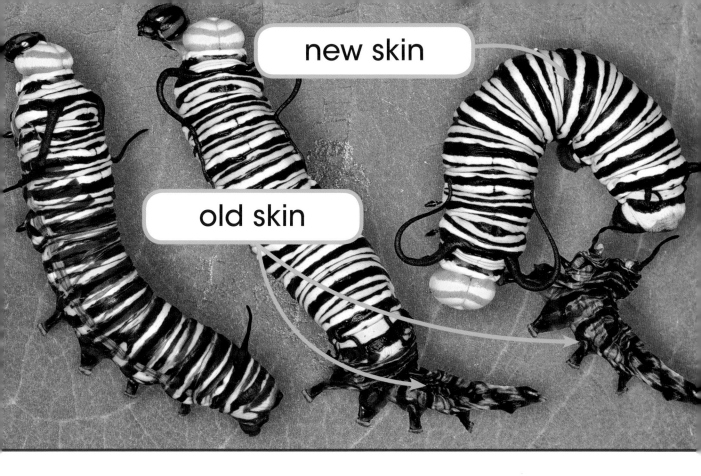

The old skin falls off.

There is new skin underneath.

case

The caterpillar grows a hard case.
The case is called a chrysalis.

chrysalis

The caterpillar turns into a butterfly inside the chrysalis.

Butterflies

chrysalis

The butterfly wriggles out of the chrysalis.

The butterfly spreads its wings and flies away.

The butterfly drinks nectar to grow.
Nectar is a sweet liquid made
by flowers.

tongue

The butterfly sucks up nectar with its long tongue.

The butterfly lays eggs on a leaf.

The life cycle starts again.

Life Cycle of a Butterfly

1 A butterfly lays eggs on a leaf.

2 A caterpillar hatches from an egg.

3 A caterpillar makes a hard case around its body.

4 The caterpillar turns into a butterfly.

22

Picture Glossary

chrysalis hard case. Inside a chrysalis a caterpillar grows into a butterfly

hatch to be born from an egg

nectar sweet liquid made by flowers. Butterflies drink nectar.

skin outer covering of a caterpillar's body. Caterpillars shed their skin when it gets too small.

Index

Notes to Parents and Teachers

Before reading

Ask the children if they know what a baby dog is called. Then see if they can name a baby cat, horse, cow, sheep, and pig. Do they know what a butterfly's baby is? Talk about how some animal babies look like small versions of the adults and some animal babies look very different.

After reading

- Go on a caterpillar hunt! Choose a day in early summer and look on the leaves, flowers, and stems of different plants. How many different caterpillars can the children find? Get the children to take photos or draw pictures of them and count the number of each different type of caterpillar they find. Back in the classroom, record your findings together in a tally chart. Look in books or on the Internet together to find out what butterflies each type of caterpillar will turn into.

- Read the story of The Very Hungry Caterpillar by Eric Carle with the children and ask them to practice retelling the story orally. Get them to make puppets of the caterpillar and a butterfly and draw pictures of the food in the book. Then they can act out the story.